LiTTLE LiSA'S GREAT BiG ALPHABET BooK

Little Lisa's Great Big Alphabet Book

Written and Illustrated by Lisa Shasha

Published by Mercy Press, a division of New London Librarium
Hanover, CT 06350
NLLibrarium.com

ISBN: 978-1-947074-79-8

Little Lisa's GREAT BiG ALPHABET Book

Lisa Shasha

Mercy Press

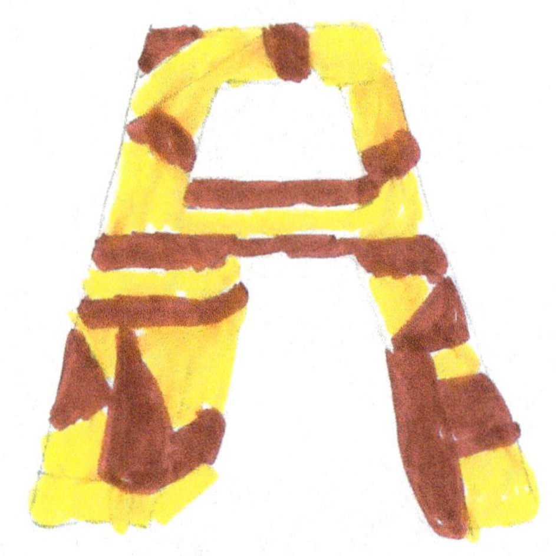

Airplane

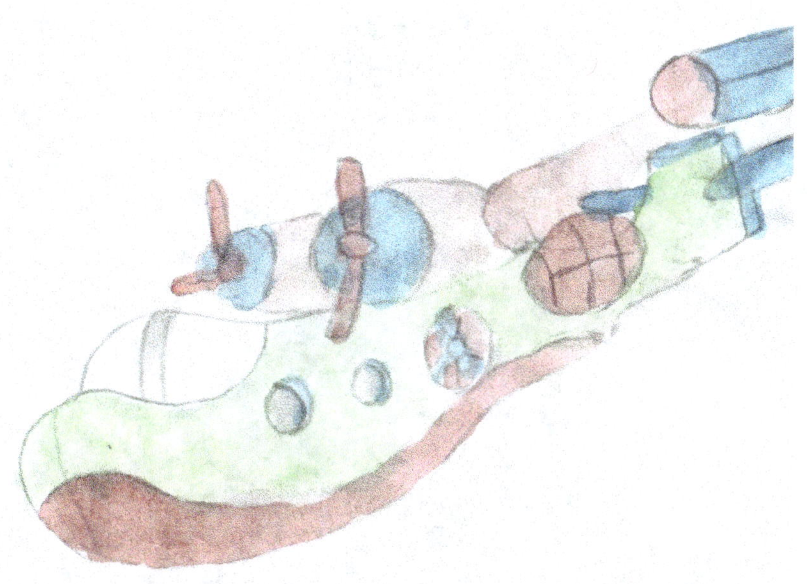

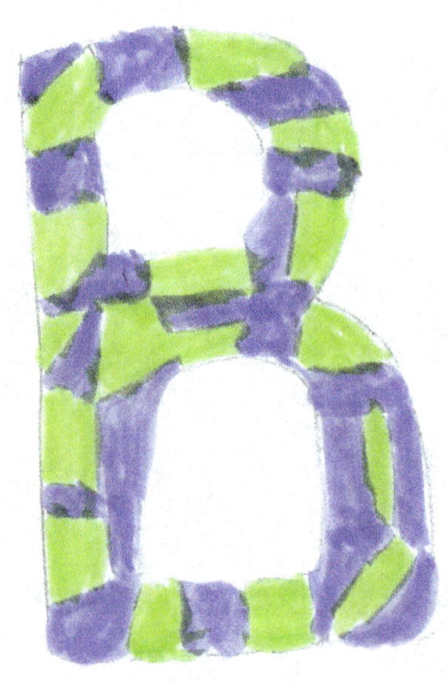

Bible

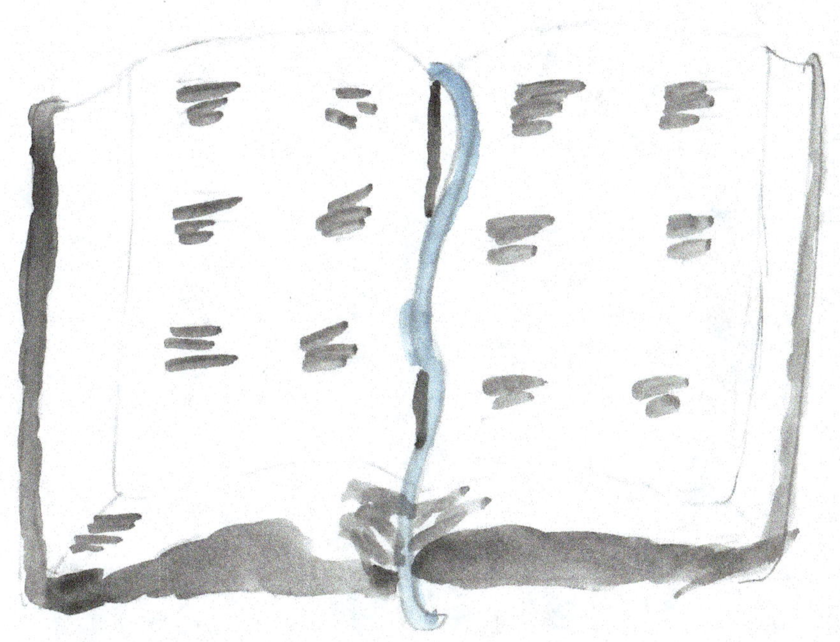

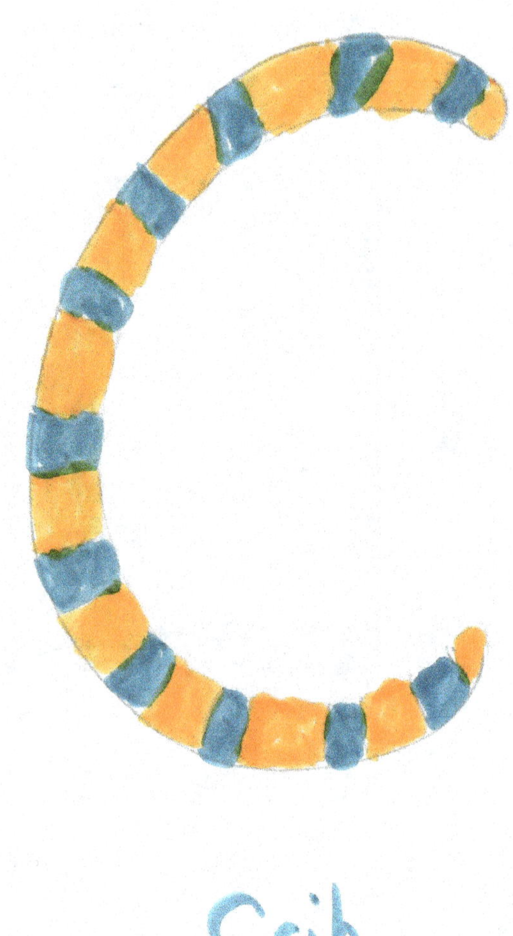

Crib

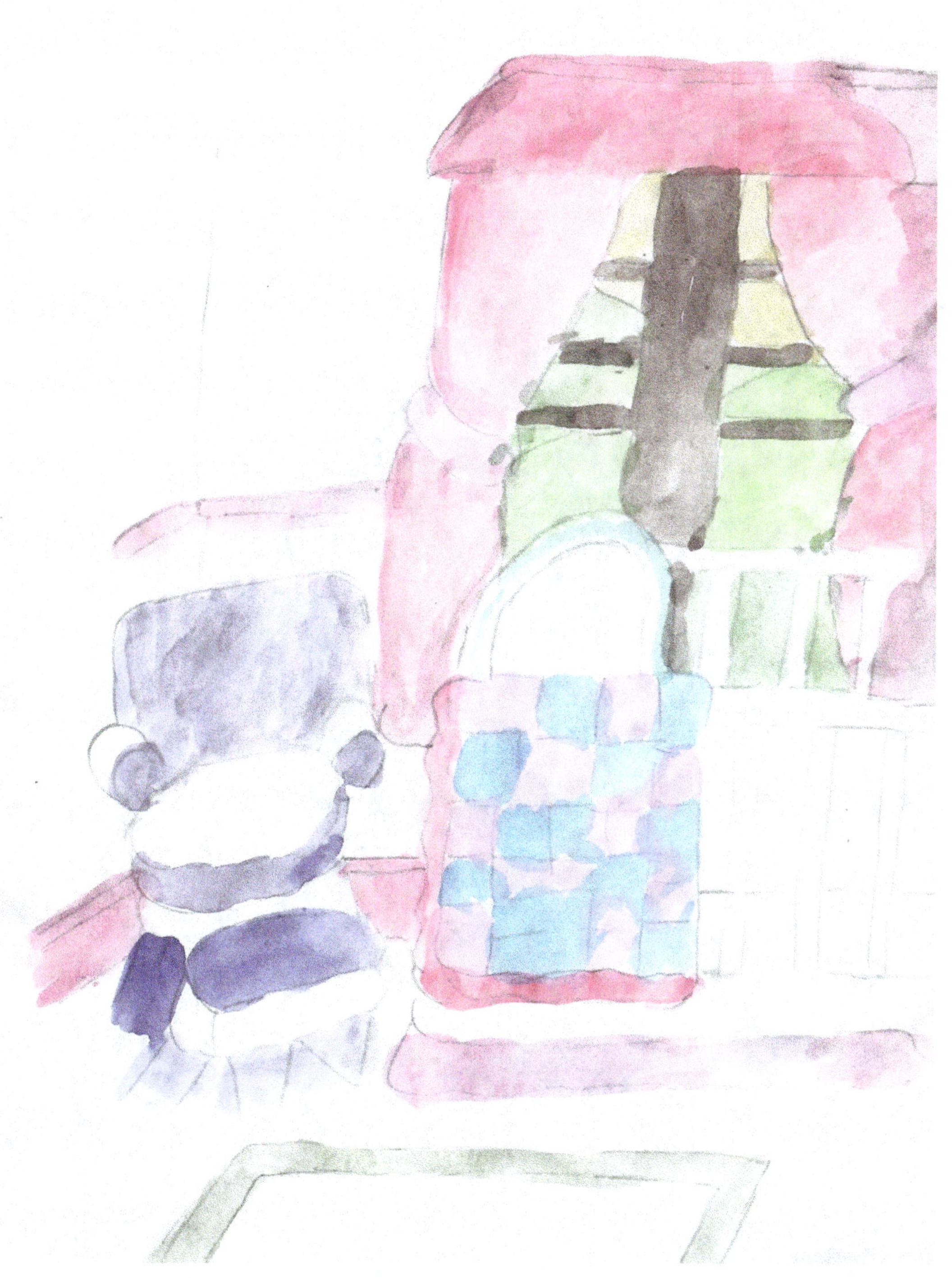

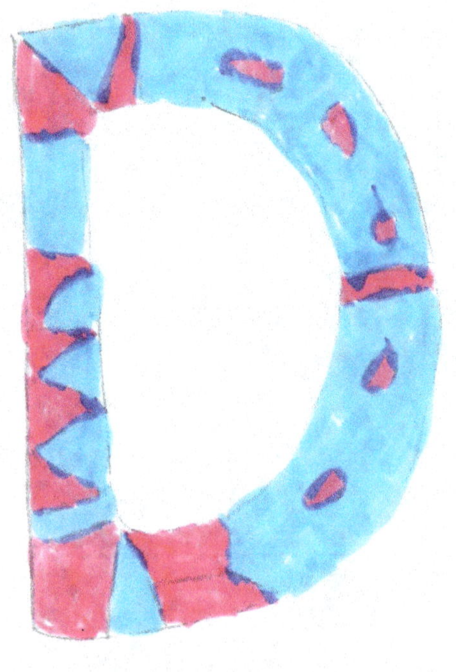

Dog

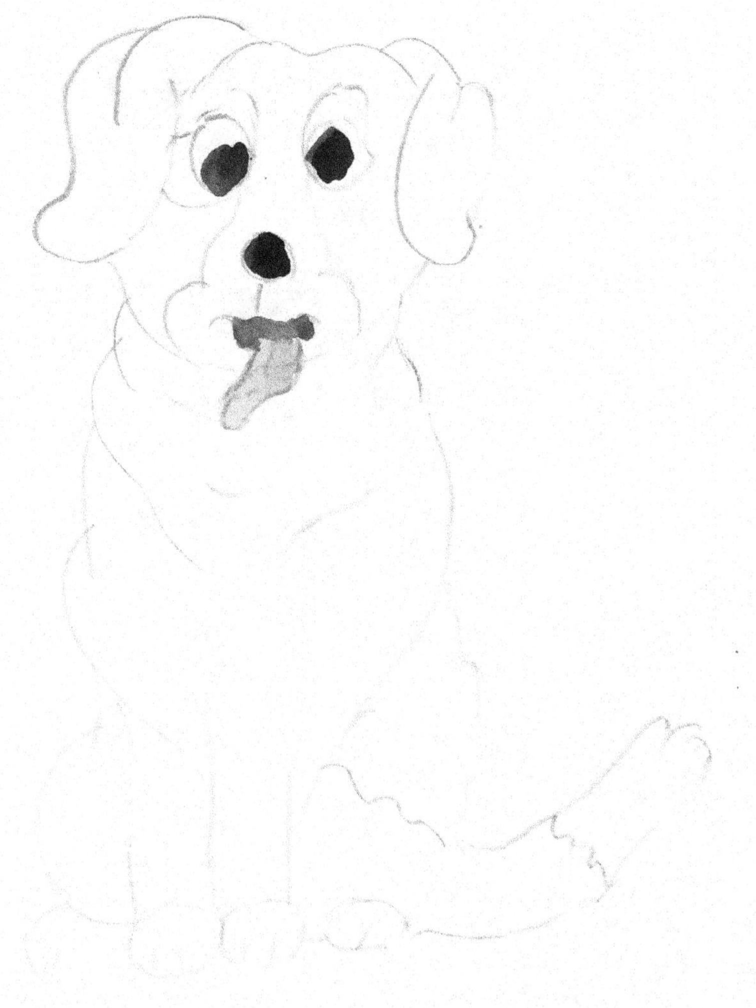

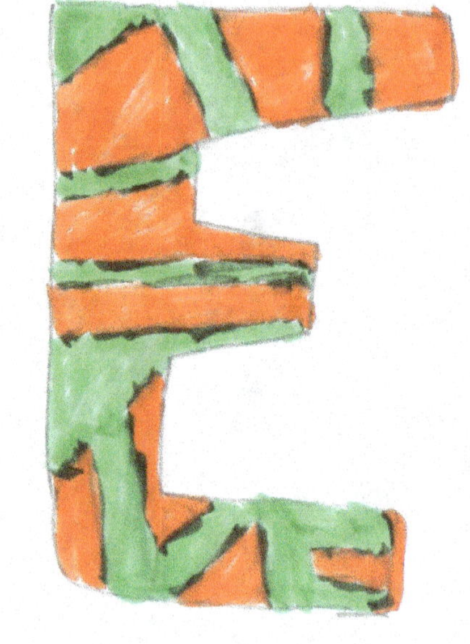

Elephant

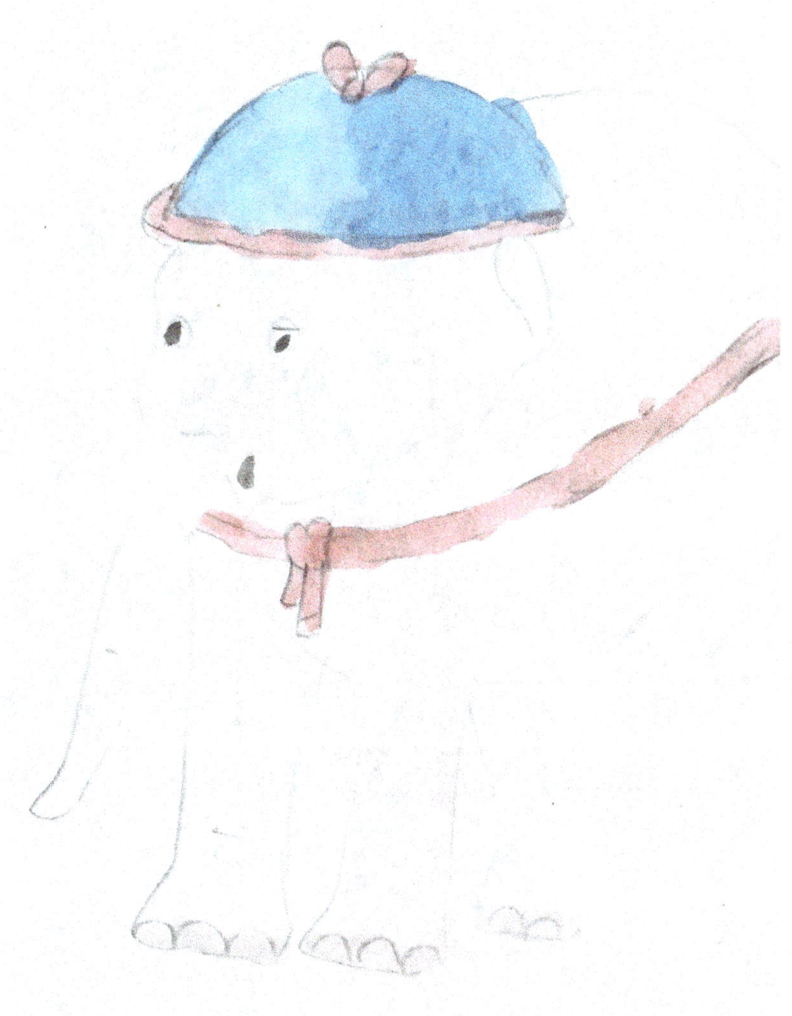

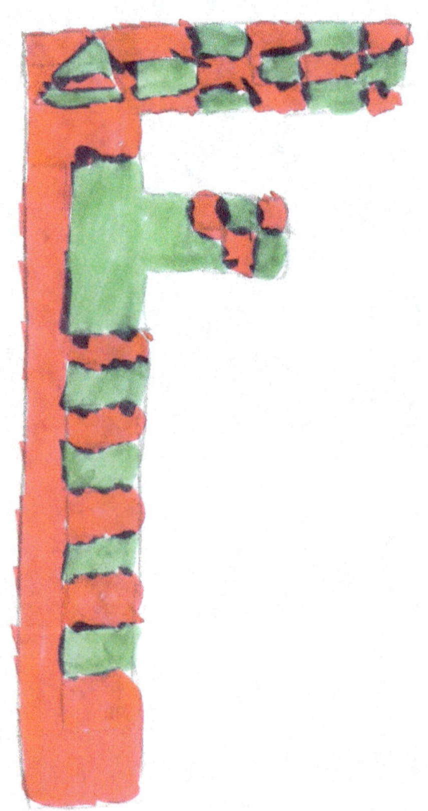

Fountain

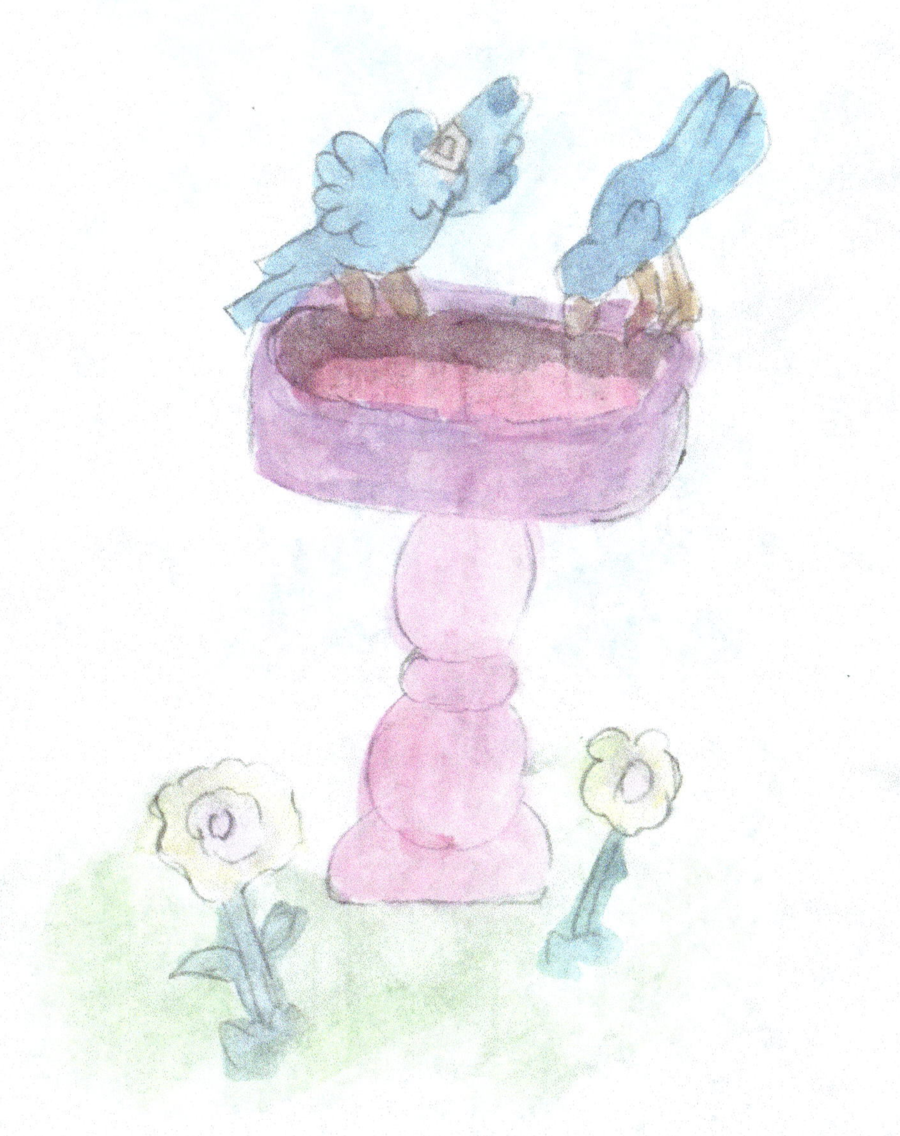

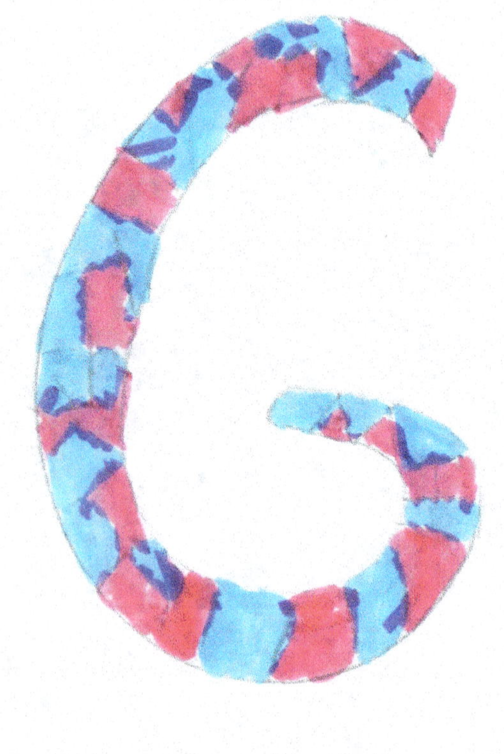

Girafte

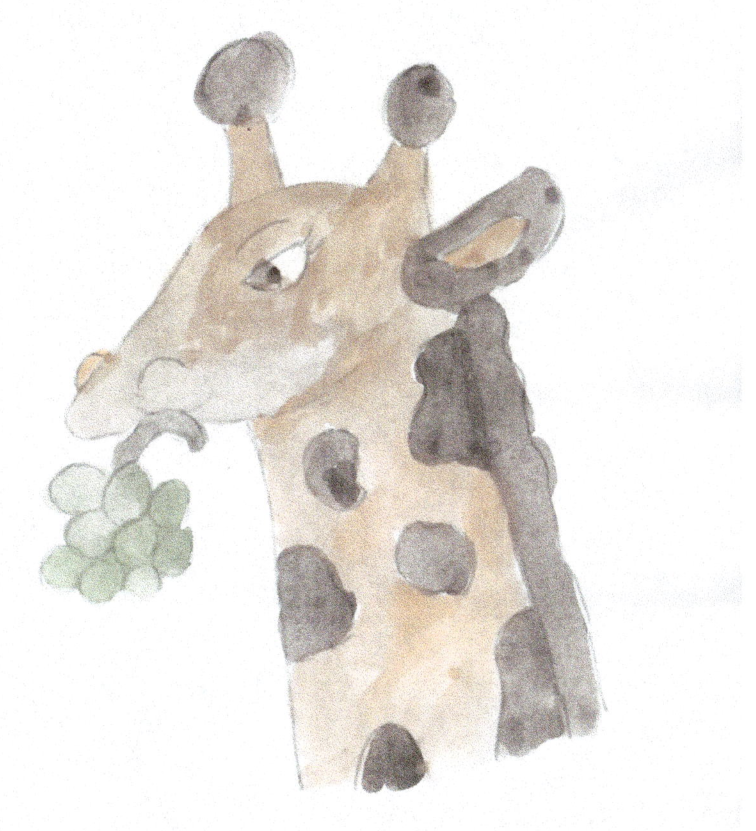

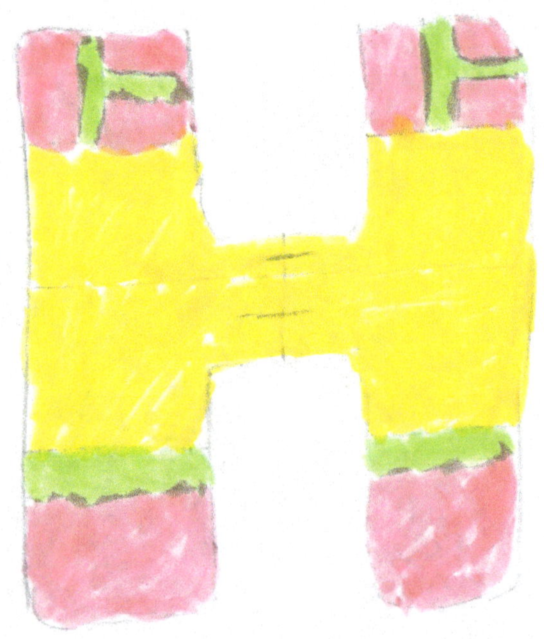

Hearth

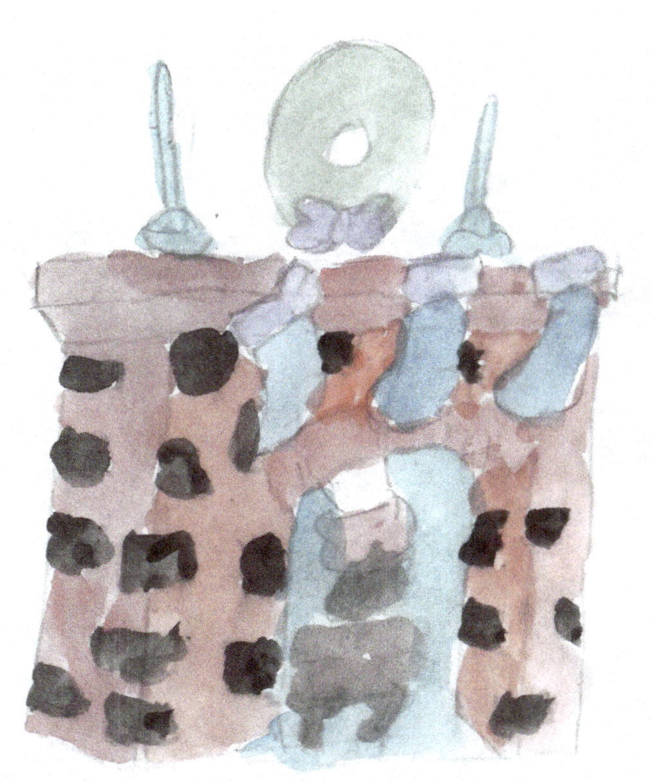

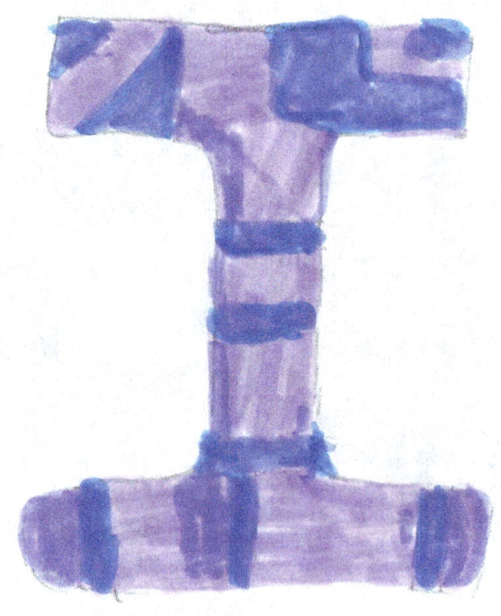

Island

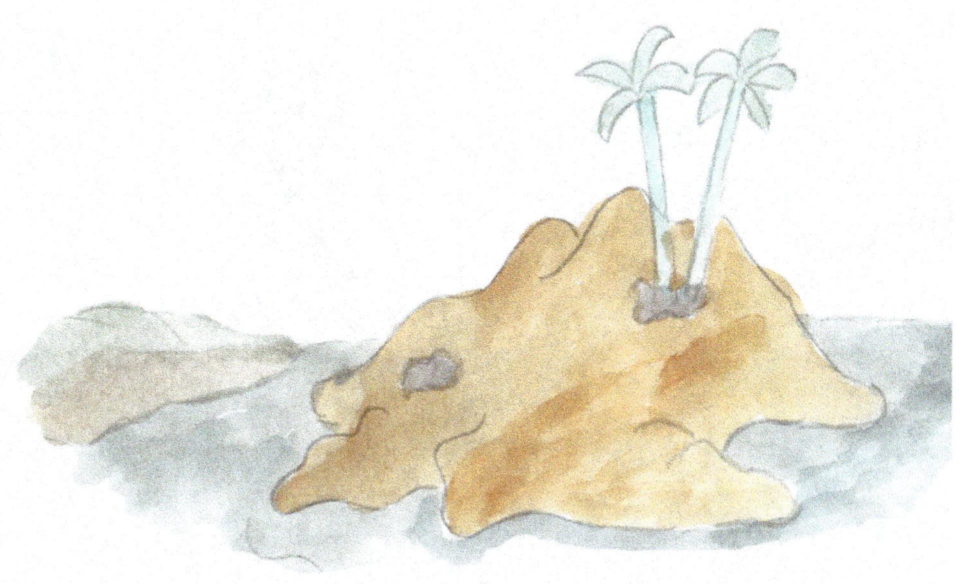

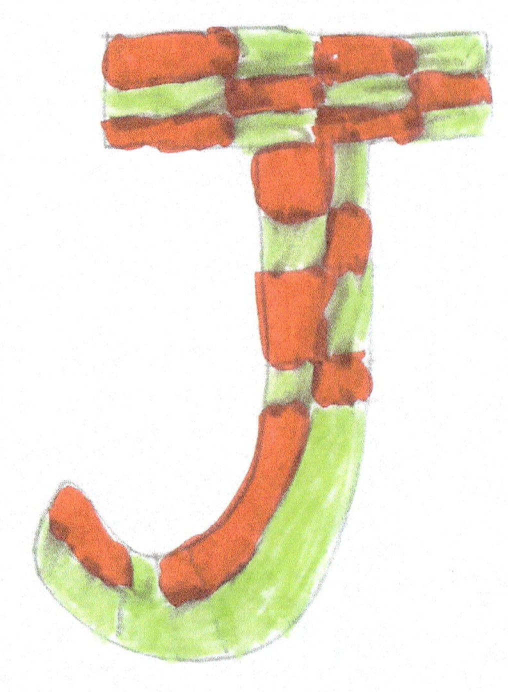

Jesus

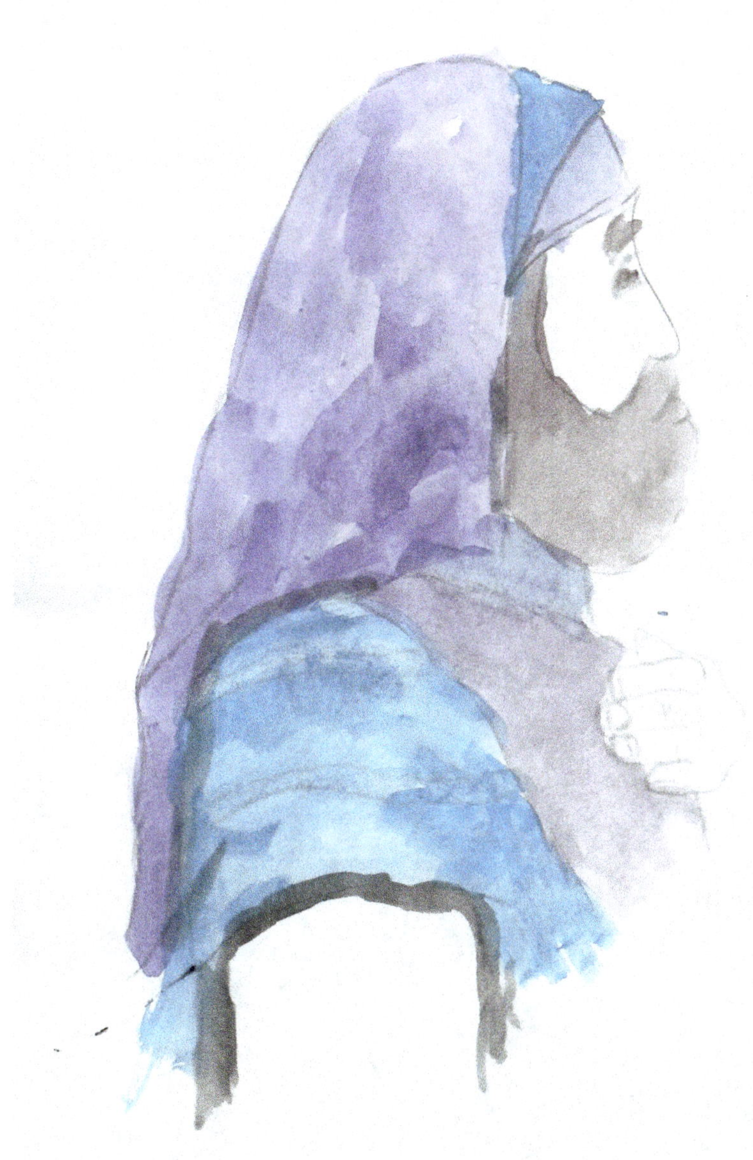

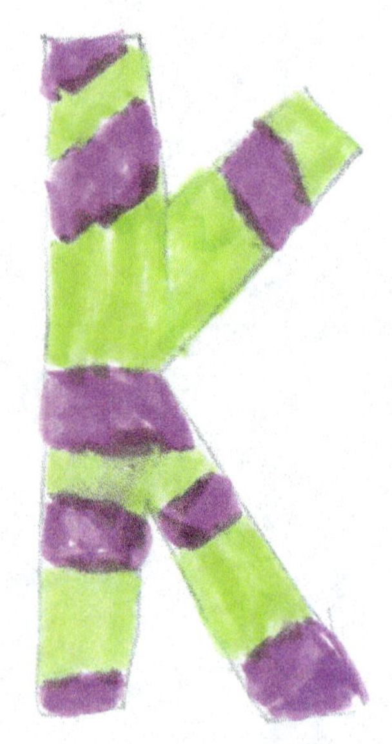

Kangaroo

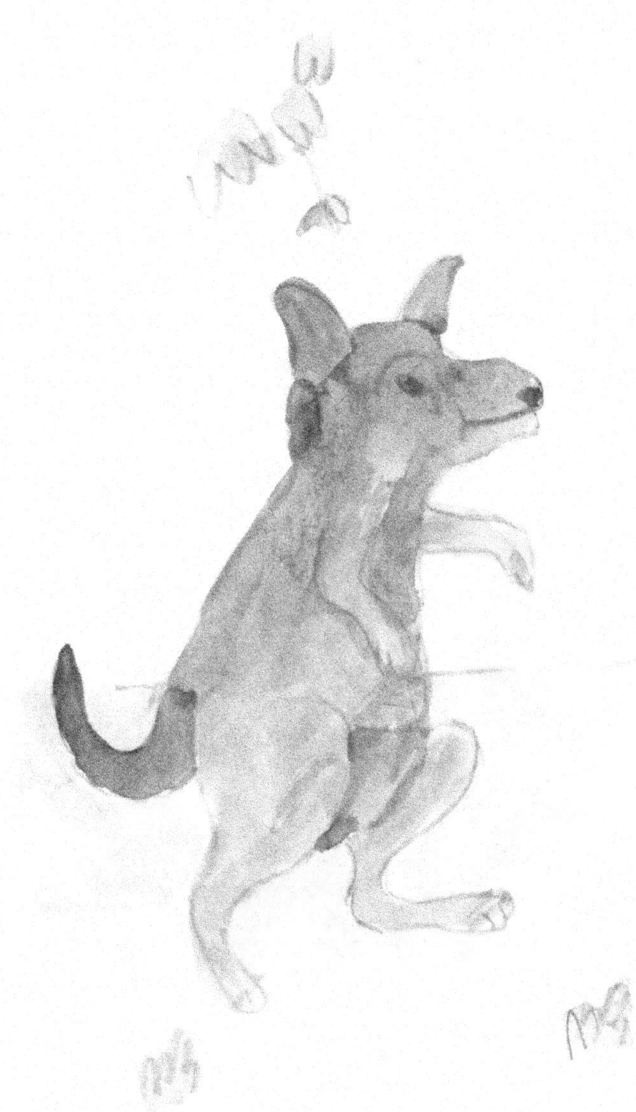

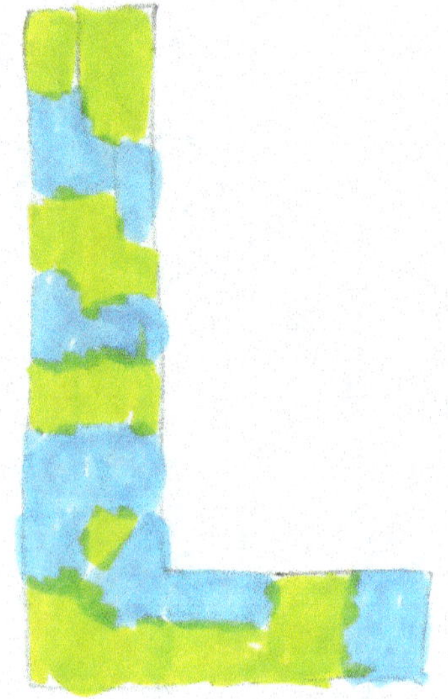

Lemons

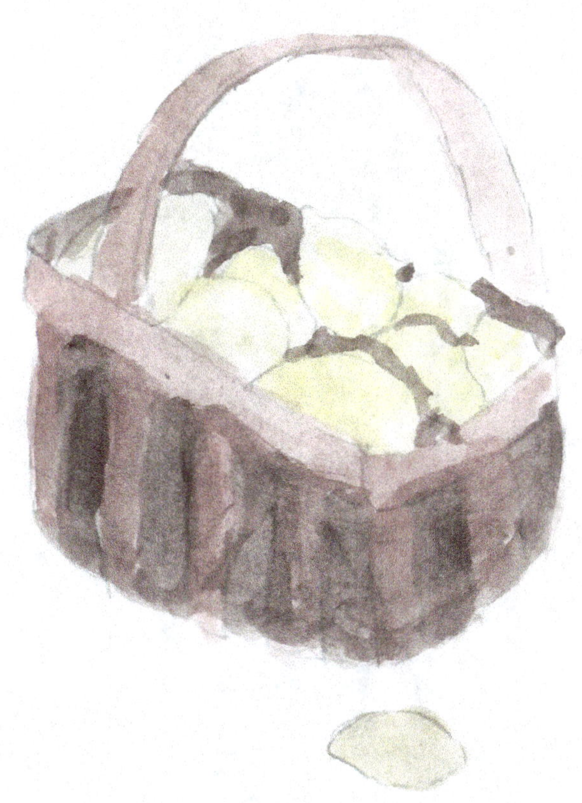

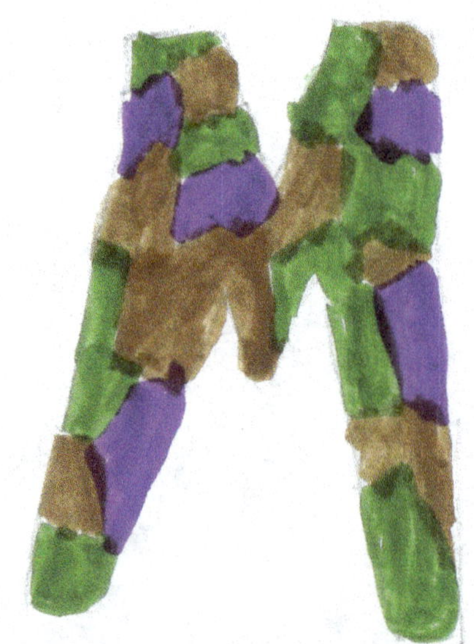

Money

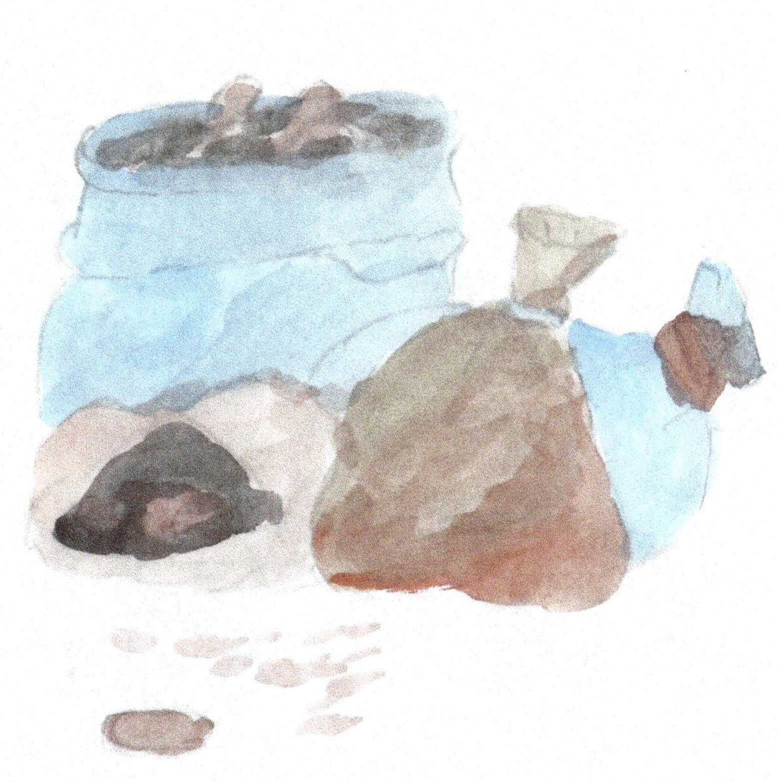

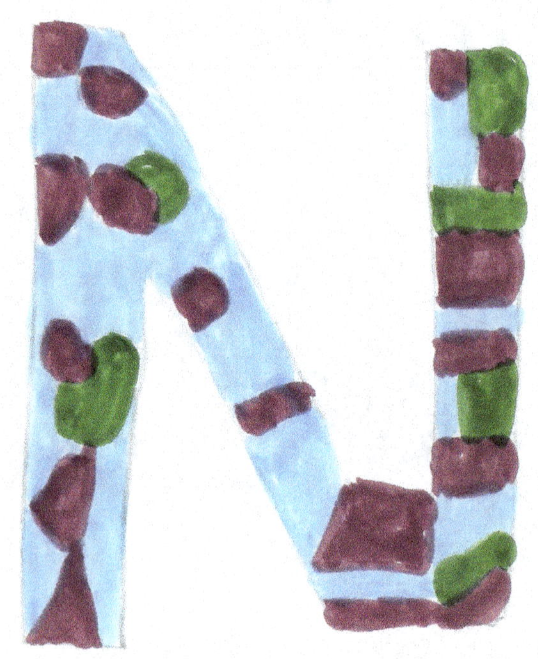

Nest

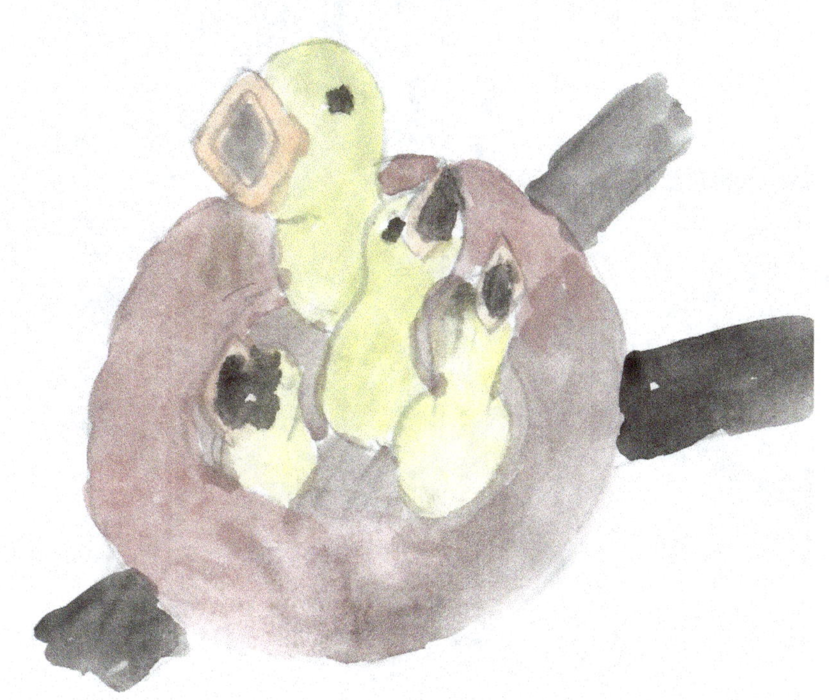

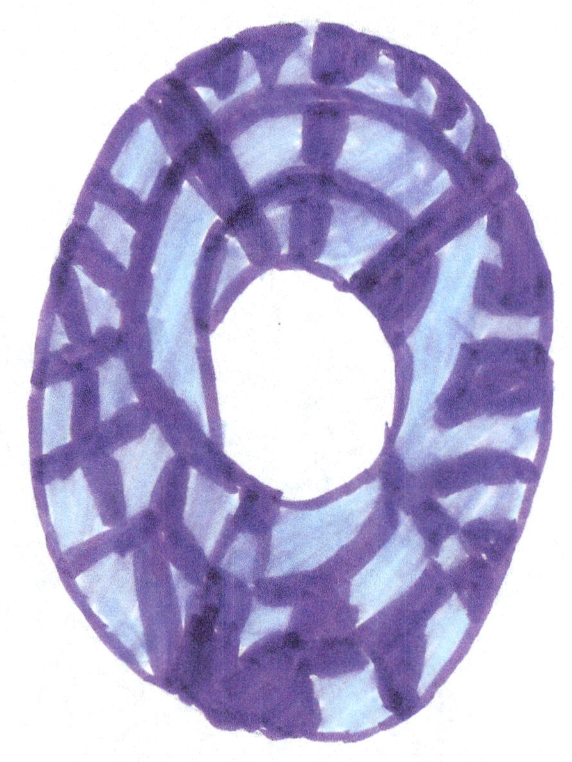

office

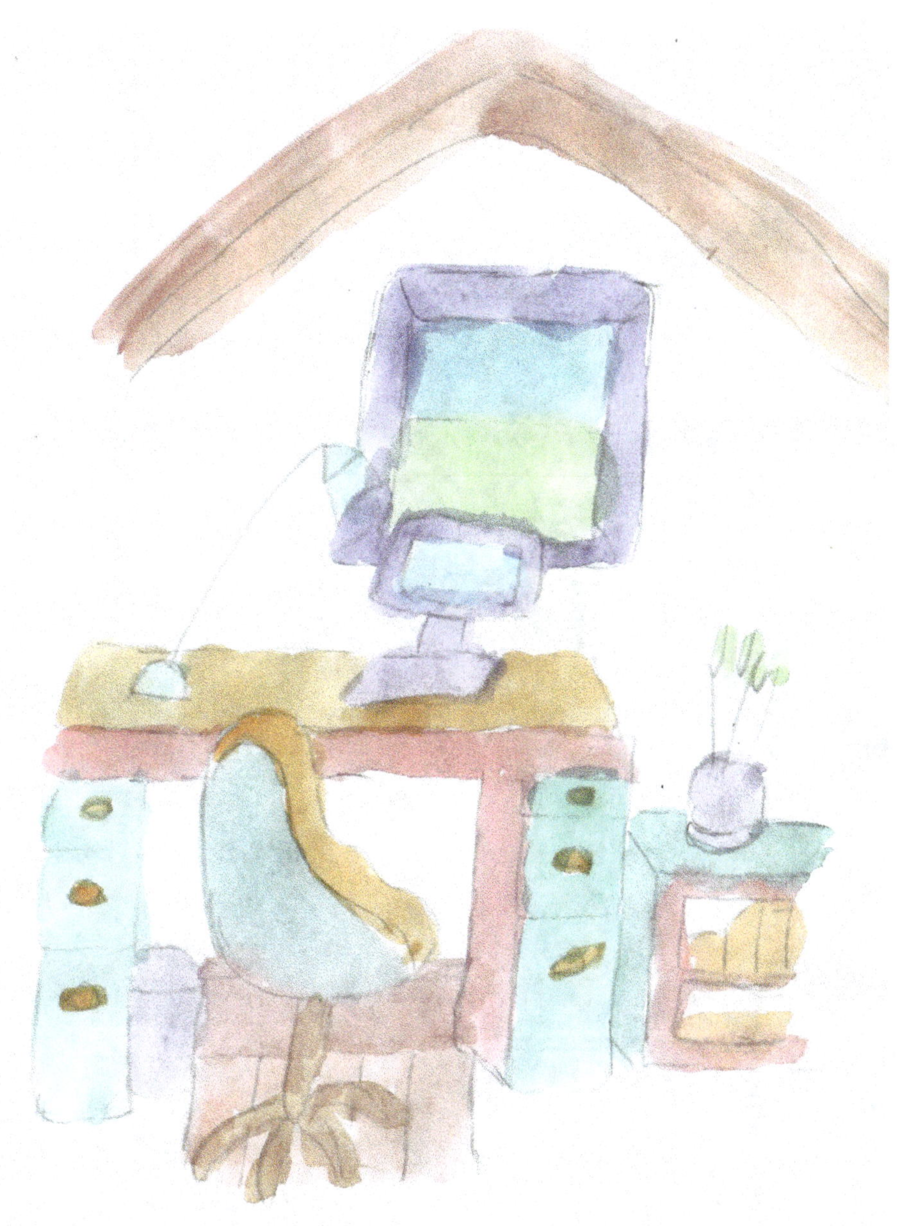

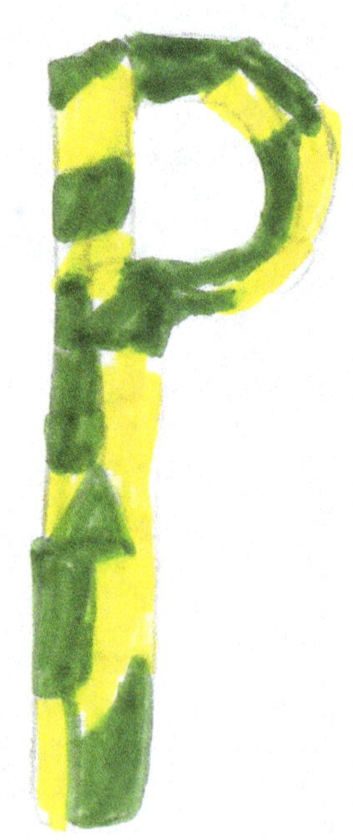

Piano

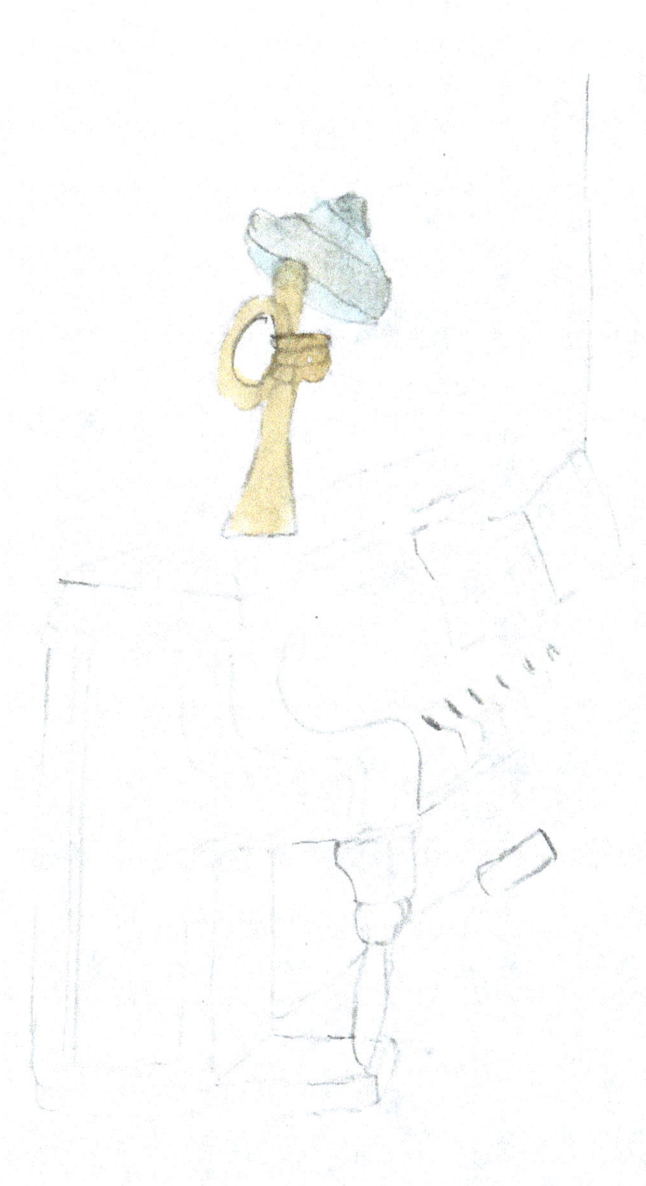

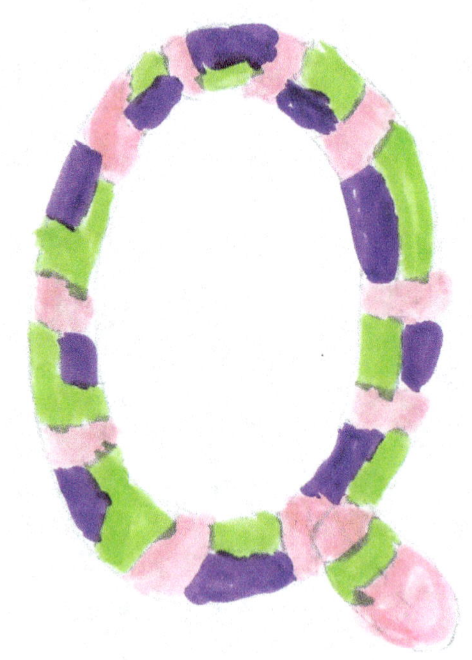

Queen

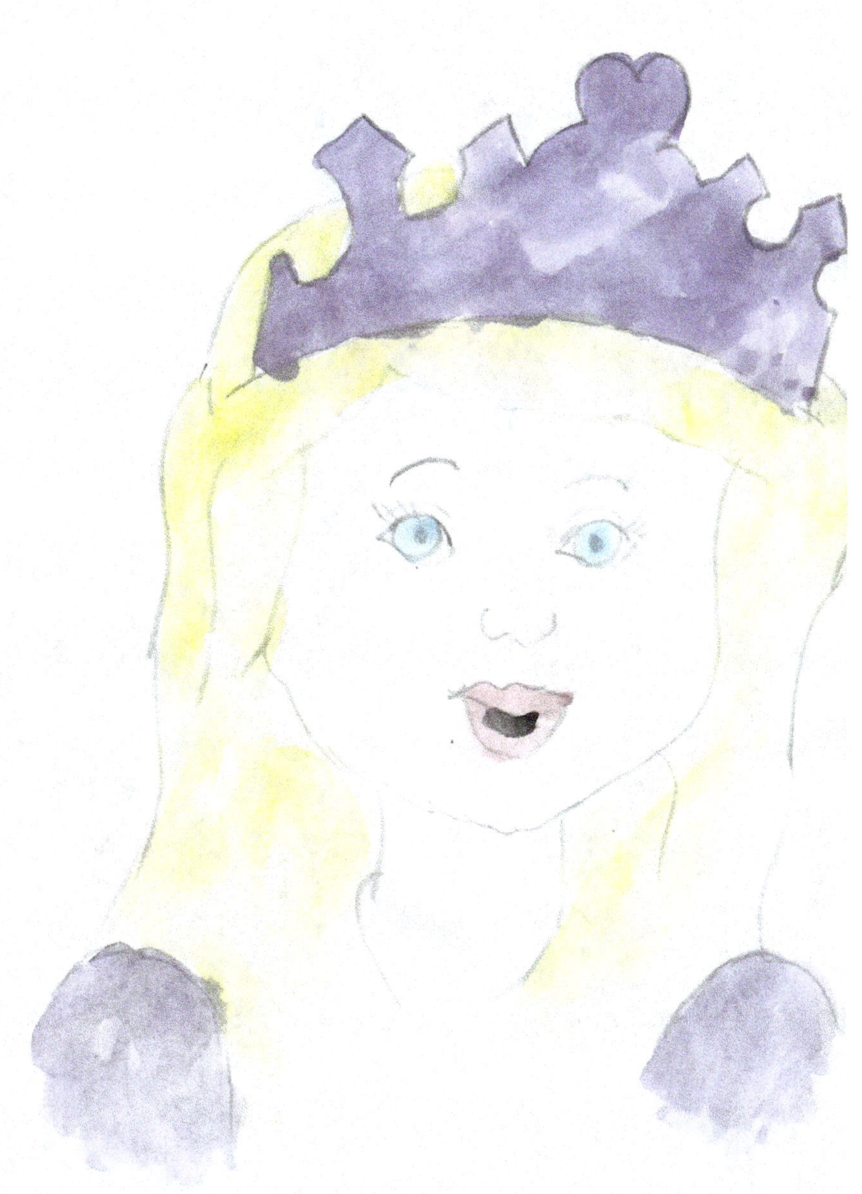

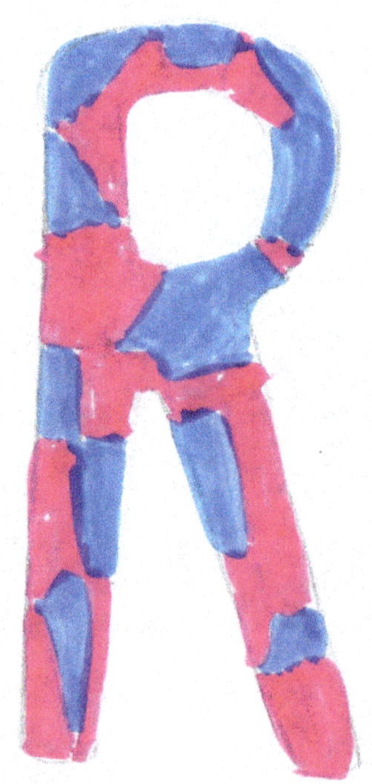

Rattlesnake

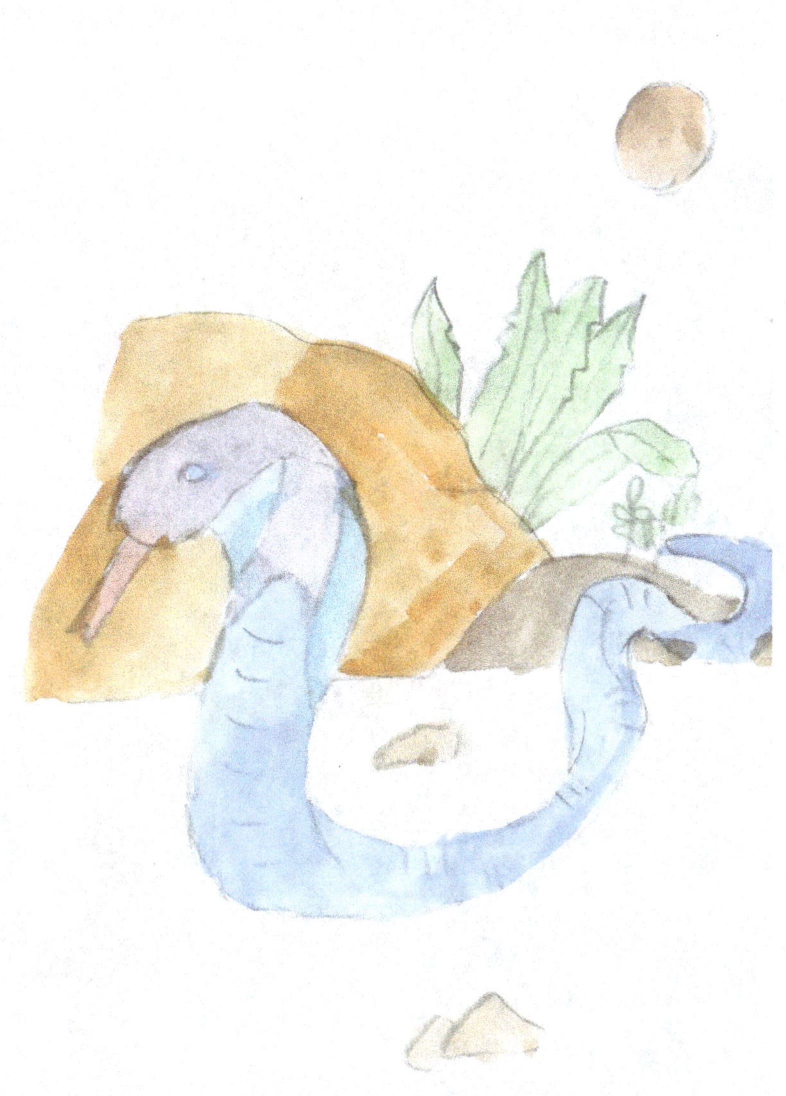

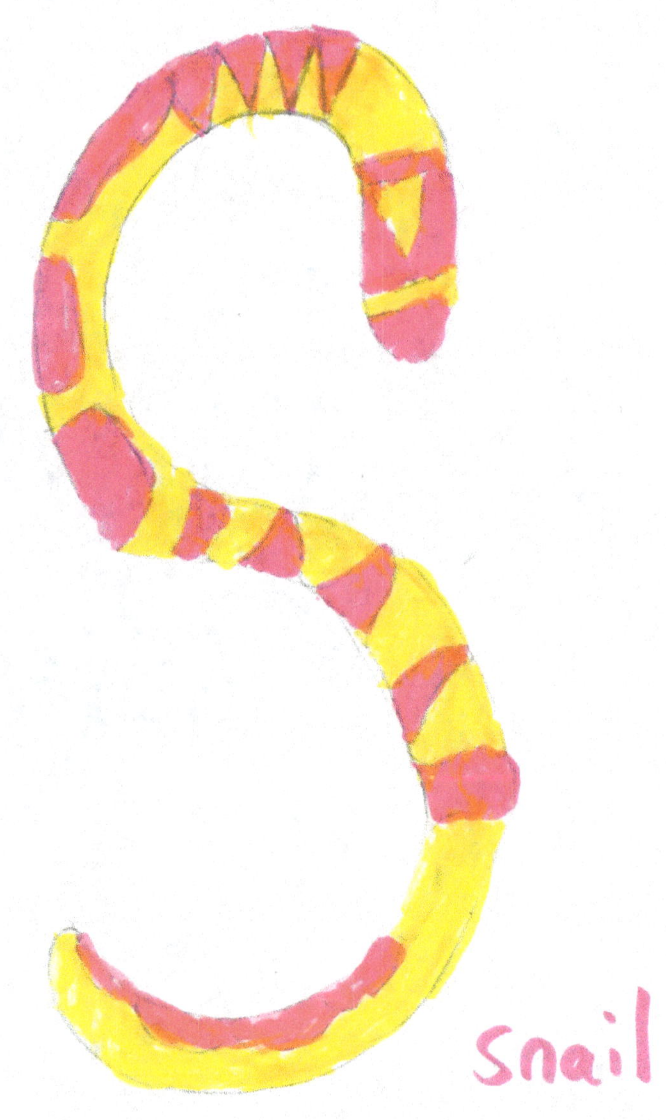

snail

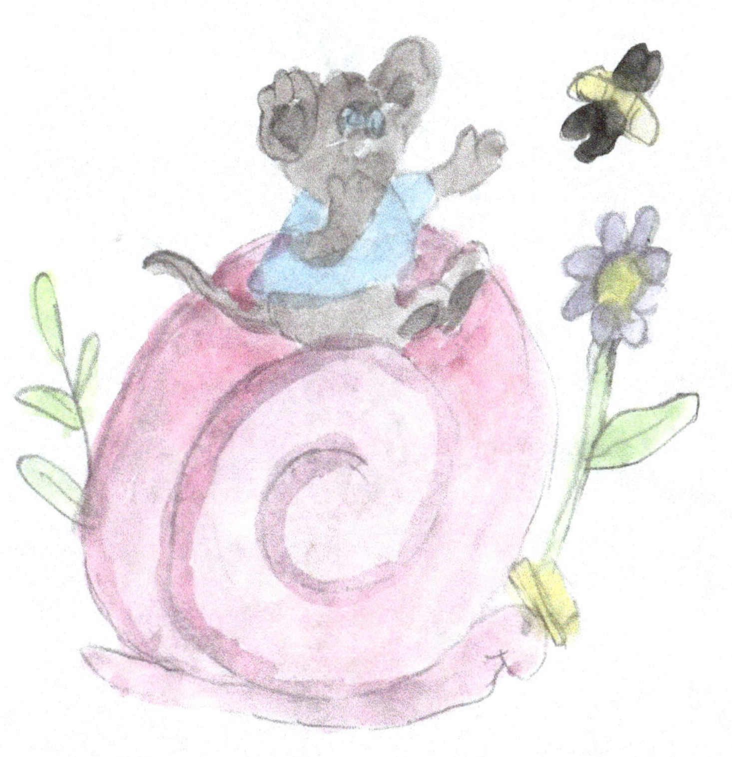

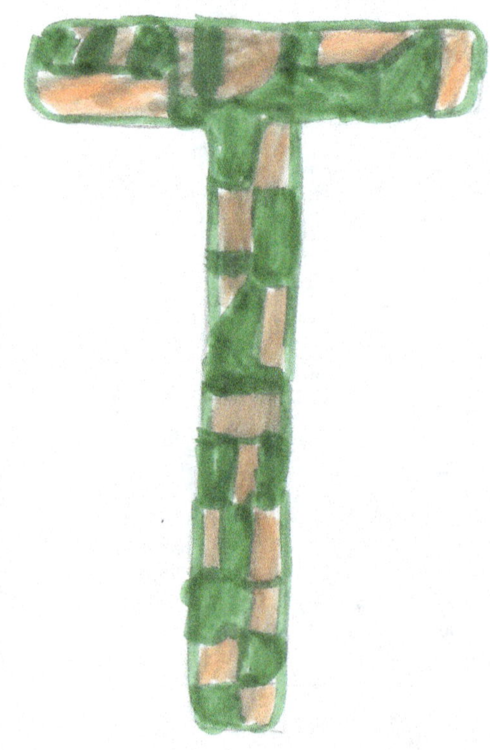

Train

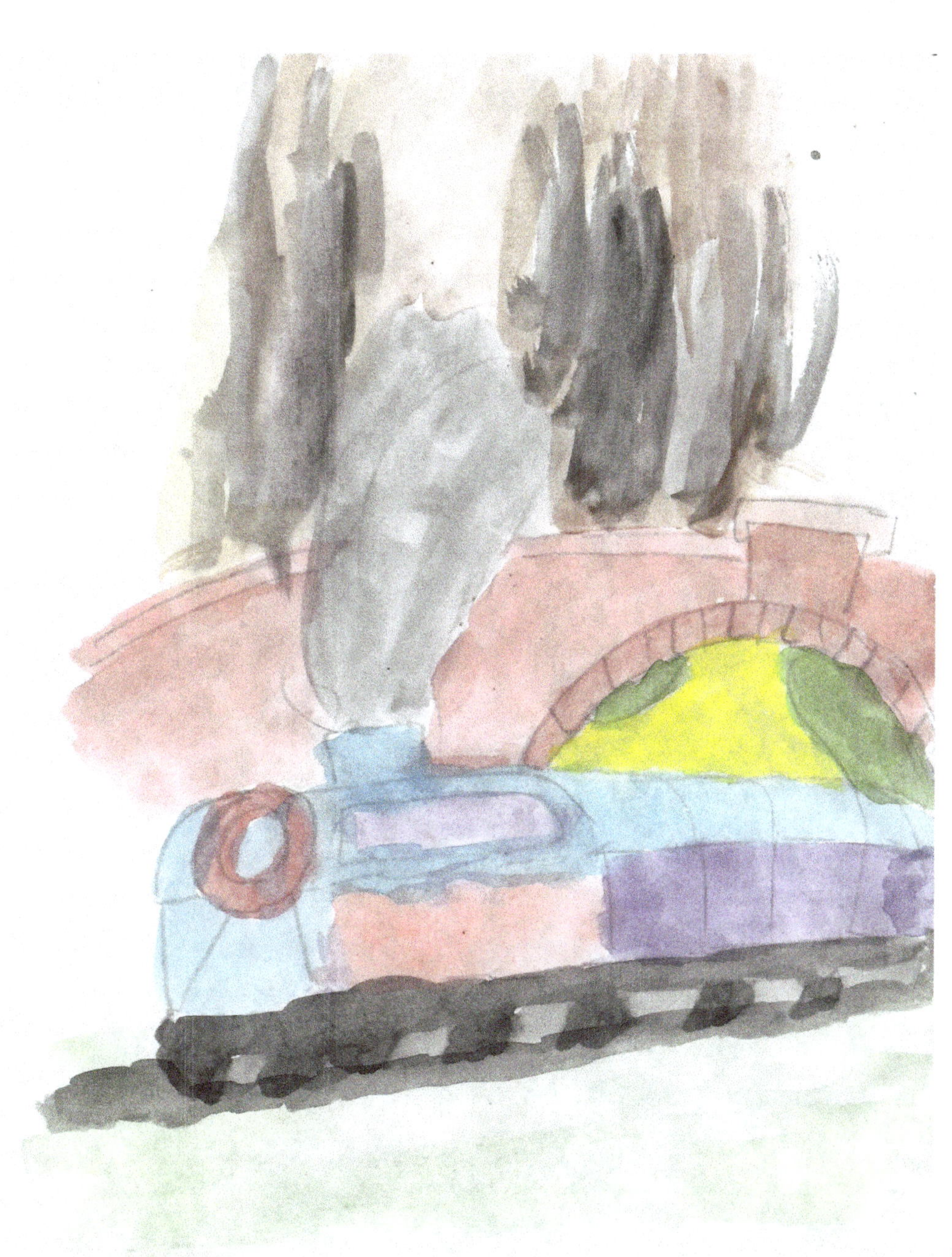

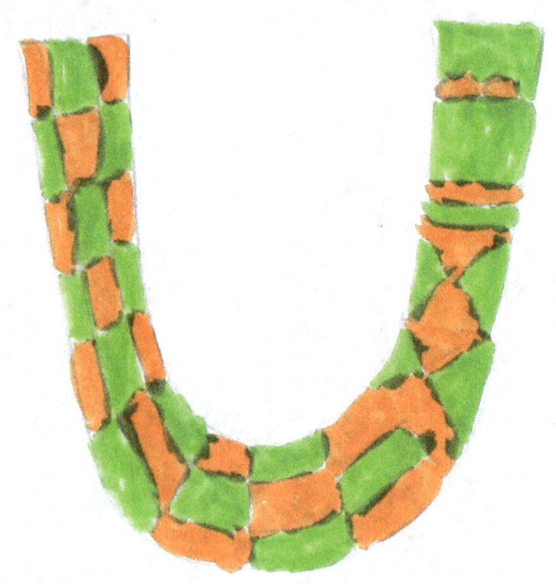

Umbrella

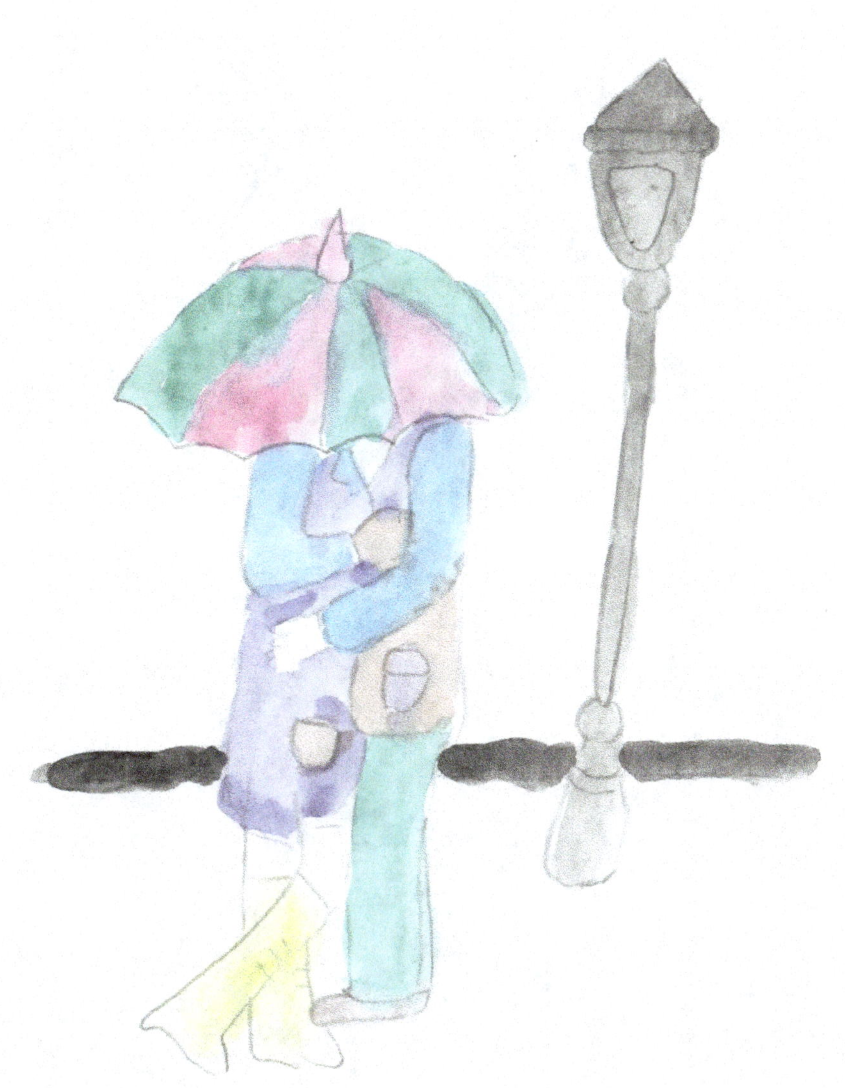

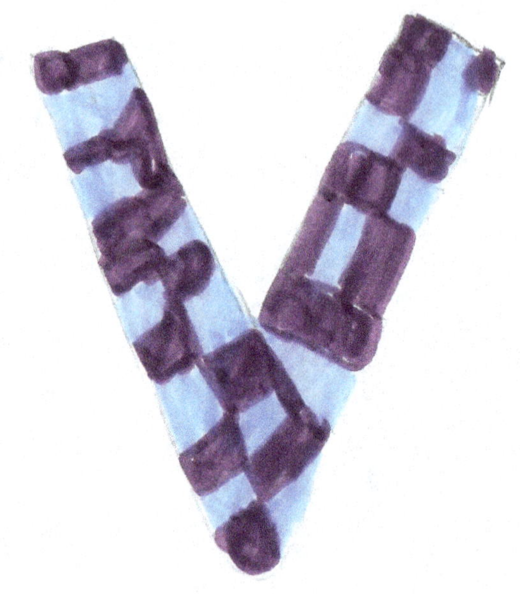

Volcano

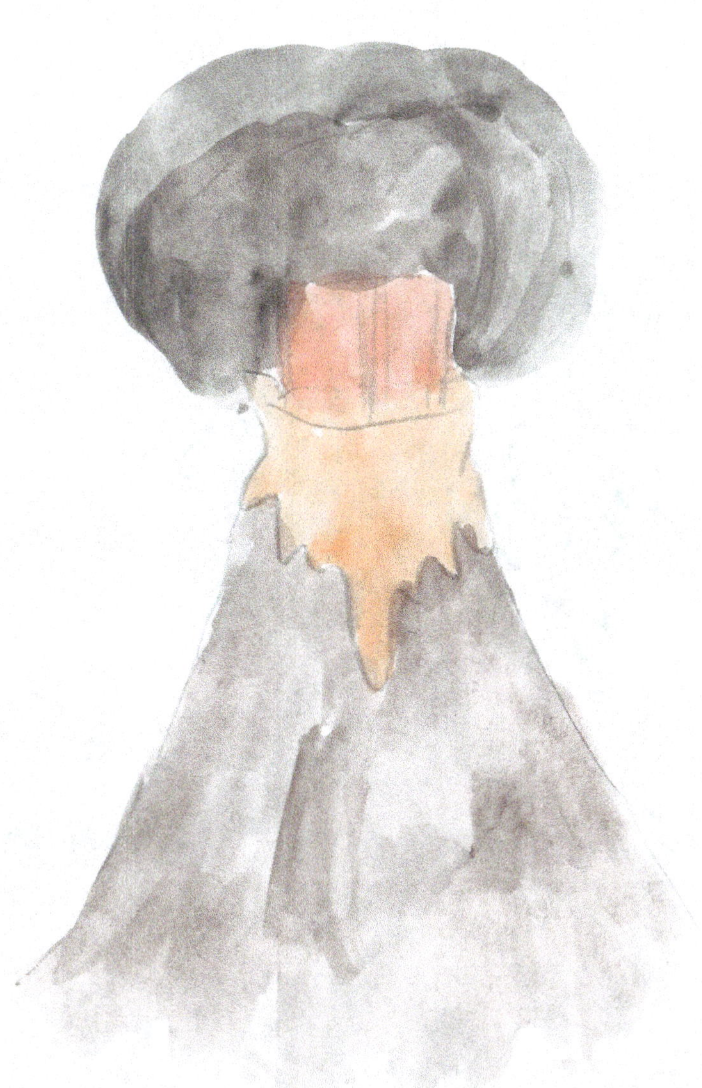

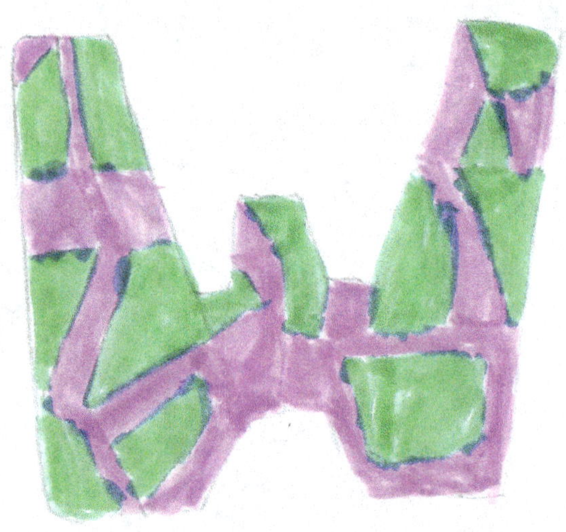

Witch

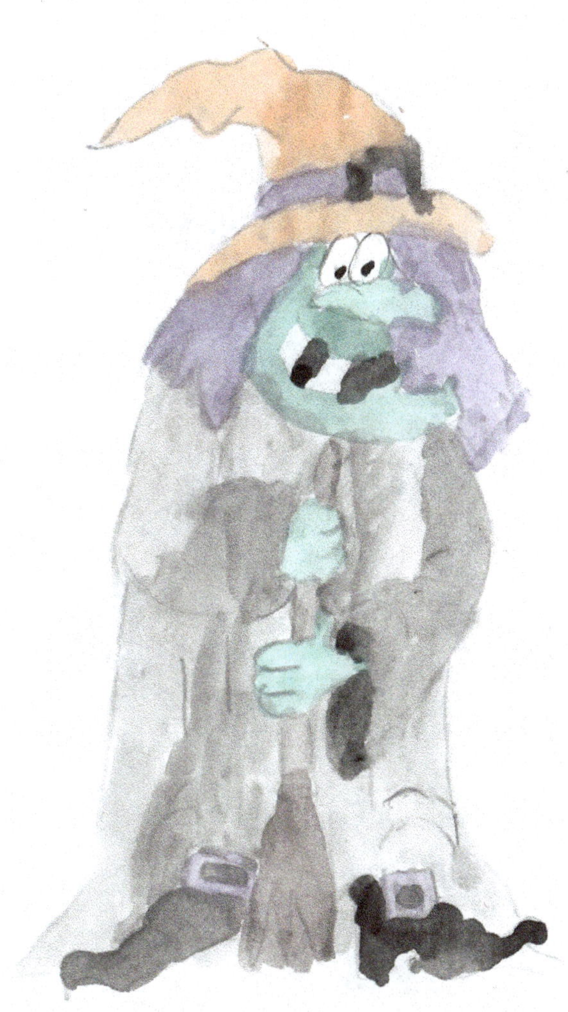

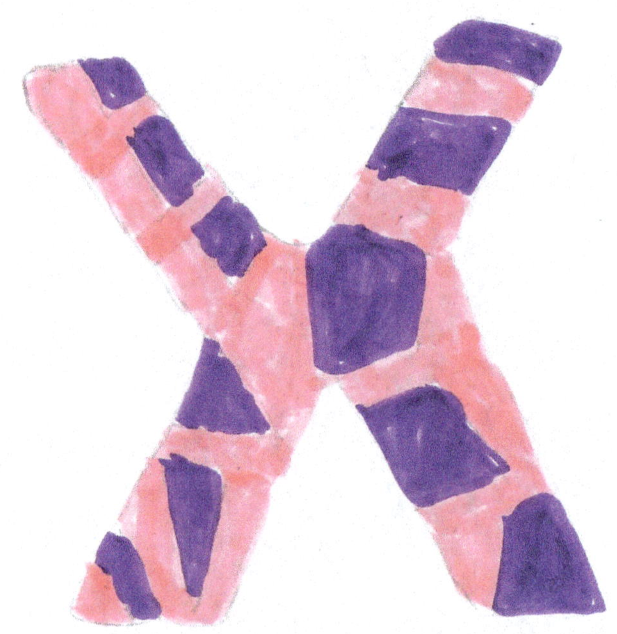

Xylophone

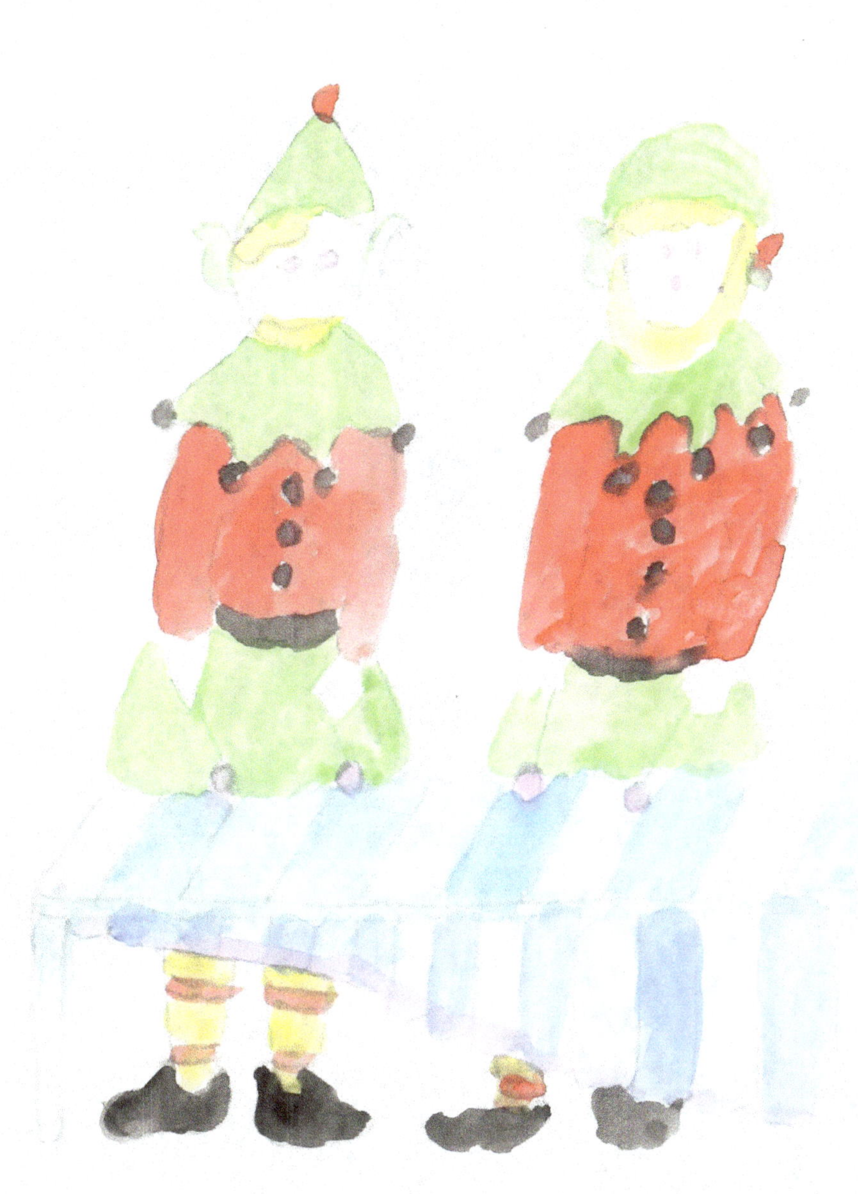

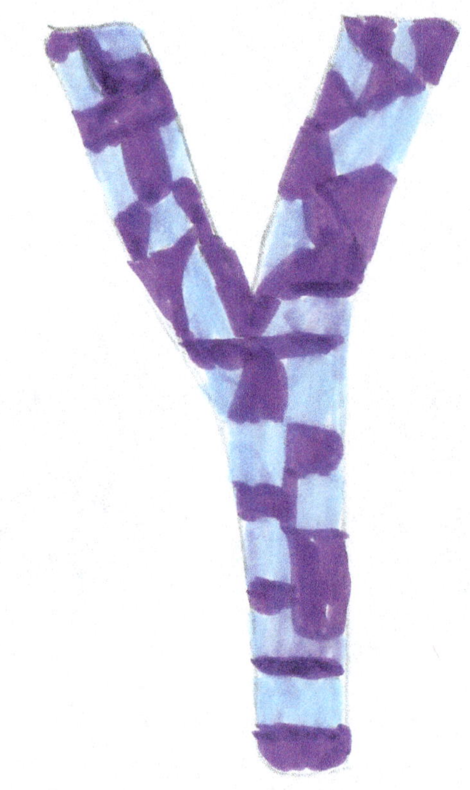

Yolk

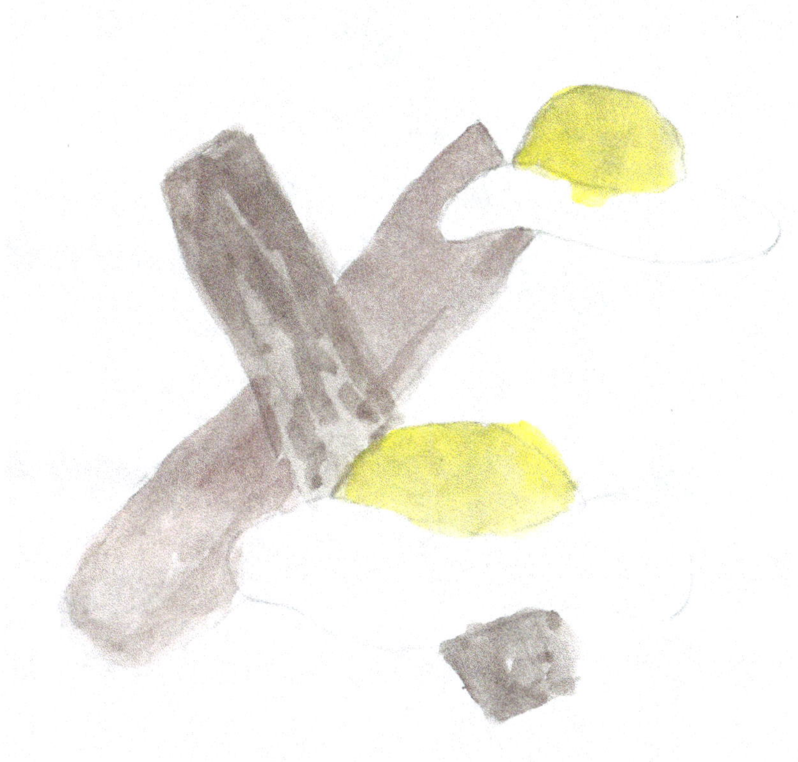

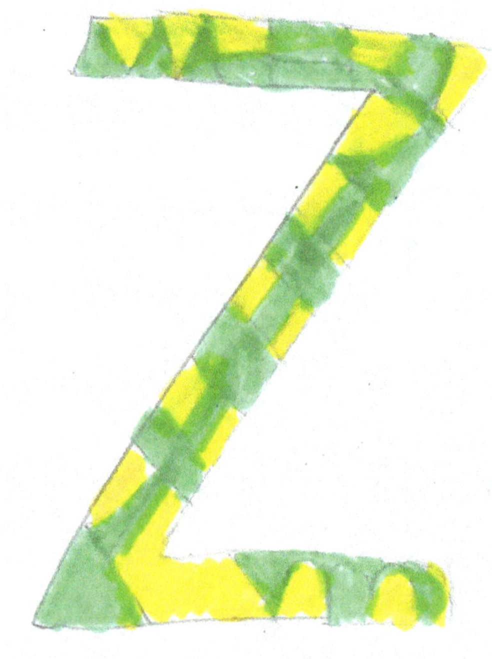

Zipper

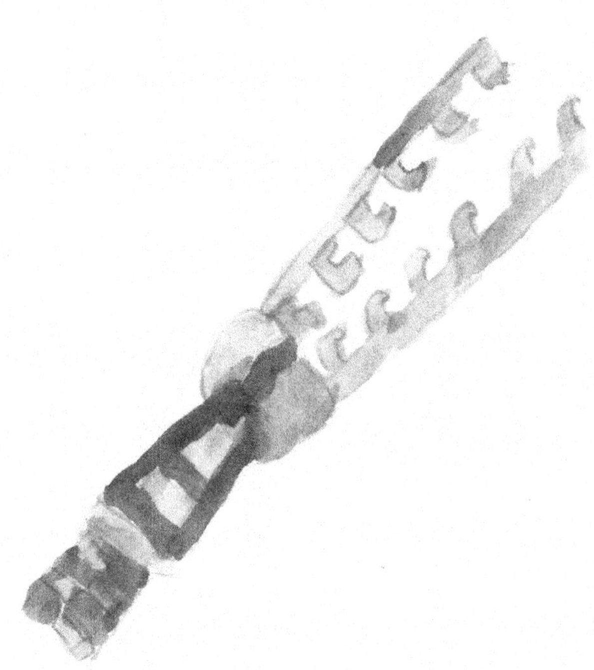